A Steady Longing
for Flight

Joannie Kervran

Floating Bridge Press 1995

Acknowledgments

A Steady Longing for Flight is the winner
of Floating Bridge Press' inaugural chapbook contest.

"The Beast" and "Full Circle" appeared previously
in *Rain City Review*.

©1995 by Joannie Kervran
ISBN 0-9647199-0-8
All rights reserved.

The printing of this chapbook was supported, in part,
by a grant from Allied Arts.

Cover linoleum cut designed and printed
by Rebecca Blissell.

Editors: T. Clear, Jeff Crandall, Linda Greenmun,
Margaret Hodge, John Kummer, and Peter Pereira.

Floating Bridge Press
PO Box 18814
Seattle, Washington 98118

to my family
and to everyone who
has become a part of it

I would like to thank Floating Bridge Press, Nancy Anderson,
Beth and Nelson Bentley, Patty Cannon, Eileen Duncan, Laurie
Giardino, Jon Hall, Ellen Hart, Andrew Himes, Susan Lane,
Mercedes Lawry, Billy MacKay, Marlene Muller, Marjorie
Weiss and Alix Wilber.

Thank you, Tom.

And many thanks to Pat, Daniel and Claire.

—JK

Table of Contents

So this is what it comes to,
steel and slate forebodings of snow.
The longer afternoons arrive with a prayer for safety
and the repeated patterns of frost
on window glass, a fragile dominion

lost in a circle of water and sound
that spirals down to return through lucent ice.

Progressions of gray slide stealthily into the lake.
I track the twilight for patterns of wings,
feel stirrings between my ribs.
Migration means turning away
and our breath would turn us in,

but the light dissolves with a spareness
I depend on while night
lies in wait nearby.
I do not know how close
I can approach you, nor how to translate
this bowl of dusk descending into the shoreline
to how a woman would want to be held
light inside the darkness, how
a woman would want to be loved solid to her bones,
true to the half-moon hanging
lambent for geese gone already south,
at home with a swiftness of wings
and a steady longing for flight.

❧ Absence is the Color Gray

*"…far from our small selves and our temporally united
passions in the cathedral of Januaries."*
— Frank O'Hara

The phone hangs
off the hook, unable to answer
the most common prayer. My fight
becomes a cry against
the slender rain. People come,

go, strike implausible airs in smeared
and steamy windows. I improvise
my own endings, look hard
for words that fit. They burn
my palate like bad wine.

Mannequins posed in the cold light:
dangerous, unerring. I could walk back uptown, turn left
at Times Square and ride a bus under the river.
With luck it might snow by morning.

Worms crawl under my door, seek
refuge from the seeping earth.
There is no cathedral of Januaries — only
a stoic phone and the endless
bleeding sky. I'd like to call you

five years ago, or better, six. And hear you
crash around that first kitchen on Cutler Street, strands
of steam rising from bowls piled high
with ziti and Parmesan cheese.

We would throw our pennies
on the floor, plan dreams around egg cream glasses
and minimal violence.

The steam
from my coffee cup offers a warning.
Perhaps today I will find
the words I need to write.
I promised to write.

❧ Her Second Wish

In the almost dark she watches her small son,
leans toward his even breath. The innocent weight
of his sleep tugs at her ribs: to be held so gently
into rest. When she sleeps

she can never remember her dreams. Instead she hunts
for the words she must find by Friday, the phrases
she needs to know by heart next week. Her baby's breath
swells and recedes the way the tide

rolls out at Kailua. If only she could go home for a week,
lie in the sun and sip coconut milk
without fear of fat or melanoma.
Behind closed eyes she would bathe in brilliant colors
of fish that play in the dangerous reef.

She lets the world slip from her skin,
listens to the secrets palm trees hide in their ample fronds.
Questions roll over her like the tide, water sliding
up the beach and back, endlessly creating and forgetting
promises to the pure, volcanic sand
that cradles her body like so much shifting bliss.

Waves lap over one another in a liturgy, a fugue
drawing her in so deep she passes beyond dreaming.
Her blood is pulled like water by the moon.
Her breath tunes to the hiss and roar.
The ocean erases its answers before she can open her eyes.

Jackie's Cafe

Sunlight slides through windows framed in blue,
gathers dust in unexpected planes.
She carries heavy glasses to the sink. He already knows
the way her palms will balance the tray.
For six years he's watched her hands,
imagined how they'd feel inside his own.
Only his shoulders hint
at the question inside his ribs.

The truths they hold in common have kept them apart.
He wipes his face on his sleeve,
blue as the patch of sky he would fly into
and become her breath.
Clouds push across the sun. A dog barks once.

His fingers trace the cabinet's edge, follow the grain
like so many paths on the same journey.
Hands that once held legal pads now wear signs
of weather and work. They can plant a tree
or gentle wood for a friend, but they do not answer
why even the room today feels restless.

The light shifts, finds a corner of her heart unguarded
and safety dissolves.
The voice he hears is his own.

In His Garden

He sees her hands as they dipped each slip
into rooting powder, an act so familiar
she said she no longer felt the thorns.
She plotted their growth, weighed each planting
by the wind, the clock, the phases of the moon.
The wives of his colleagues would stop by for coffee,
find her long fingers painted with potting soil.

He can close his eyes and smell the summer: vases cascading
with color, the profusion of blooms tumbling
over the terrace wall. She nursed them like infants.

The light scent and the lines of her hands linger
like earth to his spade. He salvaged what scraps she left him,
drove cross-country with cuttings
wrapped in wet paper towels, stuffed inside his coat pockets.
It took 3,000 miles to find those roses a home.
Now he tends them like children, gathers the fallen petals
in his tired, empty hands.

❧ Dividing the Iris

Back hunched against a sky of steel
she fingers the rhizomes, knobby feet
with dirt on their knuckles
and a promise of spring locked inside.
She pulls them apart.
Damp earth clings to her hands,
sticks in rivers across her palms.
Fill the well with water. Let it soak.
Then gently tuck the iris in.

Rain sprinkles her hair like holy water,
rolls in bold drops down the shadows of her neck.
In the East the Mississippi rises.
Each night she waits to watch the news,
stares at the tiny rooftops. Now she is drowning.
Water swallows the land,
strands all God's animals.

Higher up she knows there are mountains
tall enough to tickle the sky's wet belly,
stop the flood. Tumbleweeds race
before the storm, choke lonely fences
on land where a little rain could do some good.

Down on her knees she digs another hole,
scrapes her knuckles against stones.
The iris alone knows if next year will see the sun.

❧ The Beast

When the beast is in
she can tell by the weight of the air on her arms,
the hard pull of gravity on her heart
and her best intentions.

It sleeps inside the walls, grows by the hour, the minute.
Shapeless, it sneaks over worn floorboards,
hides in empty coffee cups
until it breaches the pit of her stomach,
reaches hot paws up her throat.
Cloaked in velvet conventions, it whispers
a litany of her darkest fears.

She stalks it from room to room.
No sword. No map. Only the lines on her palms,
the weight of a child in her arms
and the wind that never stops dancing.

❧ The Night Watch

Their small backs curve like bird wings,
light and hollow where the air fills their lungs.
In the dark room I strain to see their shoulders
rise and fall, listen hard for the sounds of their breath.

I wanted to let their father sleep.
Unknowing, I traced the cyanotic stains
that bloomed and spidered over his legs.
Then I saw the stillness.
No wishing would make that big back move.

The knot in my chest exploded,
choked the screams trapped inside
until sirens pierced the air.
The house grew cold.

My children sleep through the night.
I watch their blankets move,
guard closely the motion of their fragile backs
and beg them to wake in the morning.

❧ The Long Winter

The smell of freesia brings him back in one breath
as though even now they could walk
through rain-mirrored streets and follow
the scent of spring to secret Korean fruit stands
blooming in the April night. Her arms miss him,
each cell etched with how it felt to hold him.
They itch in his absence, or ache.
With every gesture her wrists cry.

She wants to fill herself with flowers,
poppies blushing from arteries,
cosmos bursting from her rib-cage
filling the canyon ripped out of her chest.
She wants to celebrate the rose, bruised
and blowsy, pressed against her lips.
The clean, sweet freesia will calm her with promises.
Then it will rain
and she will welcome the falling light.

⁕ Love Apples

Each cut and push of the shovel sings inside her
and she imagines the summer garden
awash in lavender and meadow rue.
In the darkest corner she'll plant a bleeding heart,
fleshy pendants dripping ruby in the shade.
She invokes the names of roses: *Gruss an Aachen,
Reine des Violettes, First Kiss*

and wonders what he would plant if he were here,
whether it would be a good year for tomatoes.
Pommes d'amour. Each spring he would start
with ardent intentions, watch the sun ripen
garnet hearts that swelled to splitting,
lay sliced and bleeding on the plate.
He would eat them until his mouth hurt and want more,
regretting the slender harvest.

Sunlight eases between her shoulder blades,
warms the distant hilltop where she's placed what he left
    behind.
She turns the earth over and listens for him
in the stillpoints of her stubbornly pumping heart.

⅋ Full Circle

When you brought home the dogwood you called me
to come hold your hand, help judge the depth
of the hole and place the tree in true.
All spring I waited for the shell-pink petals
but nothing you planted bloomed,
as though the core of trunk and root were empty —
no desire for flowers, no heart for sex.

In the back of the cabinet I found the egg cream glasses
I bought the summer we met.
Each curves voluptuously down, the way
a man with his hands would describe the shape of a woman.
Then the glass fits neatly inside its filigreed base.
Long ago one broke, leaving only the delicate metal holder.

Now I ache along my arms, across my chest,
fingers feeling where you aren't.
Your wedding band rests on the dresser, in a box.
I may never take mine off.
You have left me to care for your trees,
your fish, your children and this ring,
dulled to the color of moonlight, empty inside.

❧ Seventh Anniversary

Rain slides down the nape of her neck,
pummels the fragile blooms that mark the unmarked grave.
No stone here — only flowers she picked from her garden
in a mad dash to beat the weather.
It rained the day they were wed.

She steps back under a tree, studies her work.
The pansies look small and brave, like an apology already
    forgotten.
I do not know how to do this, she says inside.
I do not know how to be your wife.

She wants to hold him again, to lie down on the unforgiving
    ground,
let the dampness soak past her skin
and leave an imprint of her breasts, her hips, her knees.
She wants to press her face against the scattered petals
and feel them cling to her.

Hard rain obscures the city below
and the lake that leads to an ocean,
passes through a sound she has traveled across many times,
mystified by the depth of black water
and the pale, impermanent wake.

❧ Transmutation

Scorched by the sun, skeletons stand where the scotch broom
arched golden earlier this spring.
The heat increases to a hundred degrees,
bakes the blackened pods until they wrench open with a pop,
releasing seeds that skitter into the dirt.
Later, rain will coax the husks open.

Inside the kiln, clay meets fire,
slowly burns until it's hard and strong, or cracks.
Fire melds the glaze to the bowl,
infusing the potter's vision.

Even the nights are hot, and I leave the windows open.
When you visit me in my dreams,
I greet you like a dear friend, a brother,
and do not know how to tell you
that you died, or where my life has taken me.

Rivers of molten steel flow in the marrow of my bones,
warm my belly like deep laughter.
Heat rises hotter than the forge or the kiln.
I have walked through this fire,
climbed out of the ashes alone.

❧ December 19

Rain soaks the spare grass without mercy.
I come here less and less,
wait for the stone chosen last summer.
A slab of granite, an odd comfort.

You left behind anniversaries
like so many crumbs of bread:
the night we met,
the morning we married
and now this holy day
I observe on my own.
I can get to the cemetery myself.
Beyond that, I have no maps, no rules,
no way to call up and ask
if I'm doing this right.

❧ Cooking Red Sauce

I dig my fingers in deep, gently pull apart
cloves from a fresh head of garlic
without bruising the smooth, hidden flesh.
Paper-thin skins slip and stick to my fingers.

Already onions hiss in the heavy black pot.
I have sliced through their mysterious layers
to reach the root, white and vulnerable.

Now I sacrifice the garlic to the press,
to virgin oil darker than envy, purer than trust.
Simple smells escape through the open window,
call cats to the kitchen.

I search for honest thoughts in the too-red hearts
of plum tomatoes and the eggplant's shiny darkness
that hides so many fragile seeds.

I serve you my best words, listen for yours
and the voice I want to visit. When I come back,
I have looked fearlessly into your eyes.
I have wondered about your hands.

I cannot offer you the moon or a cold day in hell;
only this: garlic, the laughter of children
and a part of me I haven't met.

❧ The Kitchen Spider

drops down beside my spice rack,
hovers near the black pepper, the wooden spoons,
and searches for an anchor
on the smooth face of the electric stove.
In the morning she is there above the burners.
When I cook spaghetti, she crawls across the lintel
in a ghostly cloak of steam.
No one disrupts the gentle nets she builds
to trap the robotic drosophila
and the kamikaze cranes.

I'd like to pull silken threads out of my belly,
string them across the doors I've closed,
the rooms I refuse to acknowledge.
I want to wrap myself in a web of steel and stories,
brush lightly against the cheeks of those who will follow.

Last night as I sliced the onions, she landed on my shirt.
Too fast for thought, I jerked both spider and line away.
Then froze for a moment, knife in hand.

﴾ Cajun Dancing

Creased with lines and carved up with stories,
your hand finds me
the moment you hear the violin.
Now we have done this once before
and I press my right palm against your left,
try to let myself follow your lead.
Our hips sink into our knees,
swing to waltz time with the rasp of the washboard,
the language of boots on a worn wood floor
and a French that doesn't sound familiar.

Later your cheek will find mine.
The smoke won't matter anymore.
Then I will gather the histories
your hands have already told me
as the accordion music spills over itself
and we step under wild torches of trees
into the cold October night.

❧ Undressing

Last night, reluctance slipped from my shoulders
like a silk shawl, fell in small anxieties
I could step over easily into your reach.
Now I gather them around me,
look for answers in the treacherous folds,
look for an image of you

bent over the table
as you try to shift the balance and flow of wood
until it will slide like water,
stand like stone.
Your hand follows the grain. Rain slaps the windows
and you throw another scrap into the stove.
Heat is an elixir.

Across town the rooms grow dark.
I reach for a part of you that's lost
in the mysteries of cherry and maple.
Drafts creep in from ill-fitted corners, tighten my skin.
I try on names for your absence like someone else's clothing.
The silk is elusive. Night is another chance.

The Table

You draw rivers of rosewood and mahogany,
the arc of a trout mid-leap,
the glacial pull of rock into a stream.
You draw the gentle curve of a drum,
jagged spires of pine, dark as mountains
against a sky so big it stretches east
all the way to civilization.

You trace the moon,
a bowl of silver spilling into the night,
lighting the angles and planes that run like rivers,
like the stories you have yet to tell.
The wood speaks to you,
whispers truths like water.

Your fingers run over cherry smooth and strong
as the back of a woman you love.
You come to her when the mountains are shadows.
You come with the dust of visions in your hair,
draw your hands over
and over her skin. You come home.

❧ Reckoning

Tonight is a slim rain
as always the rain is thin here,
fall falling early
with each leaf in its own slow spiral.
All toads must return
to the water to mate.

We needed a ritual:
thin claws for a question mark,
a chalice of deep red wine.
Wings eased in the wilder winds,
shadowed the bowl of coming afternoons
coming home to nowhere we could know.

I flew east to seek a new language,
looked for the weight of bones honed in cumulus curves,
a tensile agreement by feather and sky.
Rain hissed against windows left clean and swinging.
Water ran in changes over the glass,
ran days into more than a decade.

Now I wake to find the solid rise of your ribs,
follow the path of your spine
to the blades of your shoulders
where wings would be.
Flight remains a mystery.
It has taken me years to say your name.

Joannie Kervran, a Seattle native, has studied poetry with Beth and Nelson Bentley at the University of Washington. After graduating with a B.A. in Dance, Ms. Kervran spent several years in New York, studying writing and modern dance. In 1987, she returned to Seattle, where she works as a free-lance writer and enjoys swing dancing and playing in the garden with her two children.

This chapbook, constructed in Adobe PageMaker on a Macintosh computer, was offset-printed in an edition of 300 on acid-free recycled paper. The font is Adobe Caslon, and each cover was printed by hand on a Vandercook proof press.